Creative Threads

Think Like an Entrepreneur.
Discover Your Calling.

to Darren.
Own your
future!

Creative Threads

Think Like an Entrepreneur.
Discover Your Calling.

Jon Barnes

Apprentice
House Press
Loyola University Maryland

First Edition

Printed in the United States of America

Hardcover ISBN: 978-1-62720-169-8
Paperback ISBN: 978-1-62720-170-4
E-book ISBN: 978-1-62720-171-1

Cover Design: Brandon Lee Beach
Internal Design: Apprentice House
Photo of Author by Rachel Poisall

Published by Apprentice House

Apprentice
House Press
Loyola University Maryland

Loyola University Maryland
4501 N. Charles Street
Baltimore, MD 21210
410.617.5265 • 410.617.2198 (fax)
www.ApprenticeHouse.com
info@ApprenticeHouse.com

To the creatives. You know who you are. You're driven by a ferocious hunger to dream, believe, and create. You live by your own rules and find unspeakable joy in bringing something out of nothing. This book is dedicated to you, the creative, whether student, artist, professional, or tinkerer. Keep creating.

To my family. They accept my weirdness and have always supported the crazy things I've wanted to do. Pursuing new creative ventures with my wife and making Lego movies or racing cars with my kids is the best and I wouldn't trade it for anything. Love you guys.

Contents

Introduction: Why you should read this book

So, what are you going to do with your life?

What, you don't know? You don't have it all figured out? You haven't developed your 50-year plan and mapped out how your life goals connect to your college major? Why not?

Of course you don't have it figured out. You don't have a life plan because determining what's going to happen half a century from now is just, well... crazy. Look, I get it. Everyone wants you to have it figured out. Your parents are bugging you to pick a major. Your friends' parents are asking you what you're going to "do after you graduate?" (Seriously? Go to the beach!)

Their questions are well intentioned; they're just asking. And more people who have crossed over into full on adulthood really desire to support you with whatever you choose.

But what if you don't know what to choose?

It's a valid question. What if you just flat-out have no idea what to major in? Or what you're going to do after college? Or whether or not you're going to fast track to some specific graduate program or study abroad or take advanced classes or, or, or....

Whew. Pause.

Let me share a little secret with you. You don't have to know. You don't have to have it figured out. You don't have to develop a life plan and have it printed on a 3-foot high parchment scroll (or neck tattoo). And you most certainly don't have to know beyond a shadow of a doubt whether or not you want to fast track to some graduate program. You know how I know this? Because no one really knows. And those that think they do, no matter how confident, often take some of the wildest professional and educational road trips you can imagine and end up doing things they never even considered.

So take a breath. Get excited for your future. Release some of that pent up mental pressure and stop worrying about choosing the wrong thing. In this book I'm going to share my story with you, a story that involves fast cars, fake unicorns, fuzzy toilet seats, risk, reward, and finding my calling. I'm going to tell you my story because if I made it through my crazy background and had a blast in the process, then so can you.

So sit back, strap in, forget about figuring out your entire life for a few moments and enjoy the read. I hope through my story you'll find the freedom to confidently write your own.

— Jon Barnes

Cars, cars, cars

You know what I like? Cars. All kinds of cars. Anything but stock. I used to be obsessed with a few different cars and drew pictures of them constantly. They are:

1959 Cadillac Eldorado

This car is insane. It has the largest fins ever produced. In 1959 America was fixated on gigantic cars made out of 40 million tons of metal with huge rocket-like fins jutting out of the trunk. Something about the call of outer space and the need for shiny things drove America crazy, they just had to have huge metal shiny cars with big fins. I think the '59 Eldorado is the ultimate expression of the era's fin obsession and has some fantastic lines. I can draw those fins from memory. Great car. Brings tears to my eyes seeing it in red.

Lamborghini Countach

This is quite possibly the coolest car ever. EVER. Produced well ahead of its time, the Countach has some of the most distinct lines in any car. Find me a car that's even close to this one. There's nothing. The Countach's hood slopes down like it's about to shovel inferior supercars cars out of the way. It has gigantic air intakes on the sides. It has doors that flip up, and that back when you couldn't buy a $300 kit and make the doors on your Chevy Cobalt do this. It was unique. One of a kind. The coolest.

1964 Chevy Impala

Let me first say that the stock '64 Impala is a nice machine. It's a clean '60s car. But add some hydraulics and mesmerizing candy apple metal flake paint with a purple velour interior and you've got yourself a lowrider my friends! Yes, the classic '64 Impala lowrider with full hydraulics, paint and West Coast interior is, to this day, one of my favorite cars of all time. Now, no two of these cars are alike but when you drop one to the ground and cruise it slow down the boulevard with some occasional sparks out the back, well... that gets my heart beating real fast. This is a great car.

Look, I could go on forever but here's the thing. Cars have always been my thing. Specifically, drawing cars. I never cared too much about the mechanics or doing engine work but I really REALLY loved to draw cars. I drew them everywhere from the time I was a wee little kid all the way up through junior high and high school. Once I knew that there were actual careers out there where you could design the cars of the future, I was sold. That was my one and only career path, the only thing I intended to do both in my schooling and future profession.

I have cars sketched on my school notes.

I have cars sketched on my shoes.

I have cars sketched on huge pieces of paper from art class.

I have cars sketched on my car. In paint.

Car design was my thing. Everyone around me knew it was my thing. I remember the day when the light bulb really went on for me. Somehow I saw an ad for this course where someone would teach you how to design cars. It included a long fold-out car design sketch (done in blue ink), and an instructional VHS tape (It's like a brick that plays a video) with sketching and rendering instructions on the process. My parents ordered it for me in the mail and when it came I just about lost my mind. I can't remember the person or name of it but to that guy, wherever you are, thanks a bunch. That's when I felt the feeling of being a car designer.

Car designer. It made sense to pursue this as a profession. I remember in High School sitting in class hearing about applying to colleges and deciding on a major and just not connecting with the struggle. Why? Because there are only 2 or 3 automotive design schools in the country and the major is, well... automotive design.

I had 1 major in mind. I applied to 1 school. 1 time.

No back up plan, no other schools to pursue, no other majors of interest. But you know what? I got in. I was accepted. Easy as pie!

Now if you're reading this far you've got to be

wondering if you just got tricked. "Isn't this a book about not knowing what you want? This guy seems like he has it all figured out!" Don't worry, I'll break everything down in the next chapter.

Keep reading.

SUMMARY: Some people have a "thing" and others don't. That's ok.

BRAIN DUMP: What do your friends and family think you're good at? Have they suggested careers or majors that they think would be a good fit for you? If so, what?

I'm going to college!

Remember in the introduction where I mentioned fuzzy toilet seats? I'll tell that story to you here in this chapter, just wait for it. But first, the wonderful world of college. Now you may have gone through (or be going through), a much bigger set of decisions and stress about choosing a school, paying for school, room and board, etc. Depending on how early your parents started saving for college, your budget, what's in your home state, etc., you may have a much different pathway to your particular school. Or you may be hitting pause on the college thing or skipping it altogether. That's ok.

There are few experiences you'll ever have that are as exciting and nerve-wracking as college. You'll move in all your junk to your dorm room, your parents will cry and take awkward pictures of you in front of the school sign, they'll drive away, you'll take a breath and then say to yourself...

WHAT. AM. I. DOING?

Here's the bottom line about college. It's amazing. Overnight you are suddenly a new version of you; a new, singular, responsible, independent, double-the-awesome version of you. Instantly. Now for some, this is empowering. You are going to do great with your newfound freedom and really come into your own, step into a new version of your life with poise. For others, this can be a hard time. Without anything connecting you back to the home and life you've known your entire life, you kind of freak out.

And that's to be expected. But here's the thing about college. You have to push through the freak outs to get to the good stuff. And you'll do it quickly, don't worry. Here are just a few memories and experiences that I had during my first few months at art school, a good 800 miles away from my parents and every other human being on the earth that already knew me.

I remember going to art school thinking I was "the best" at drawing cars. Because out of everyone in my high school, I was the best. But ten minutes into my first class I met about 20 other students exactly my age who were about 1000 times better than me. Reality check. I was not the best car artist on the planet. In fact, I felt like my work was junk. That was a tough day.

At my art school we had apartments instead of dorm rooms. I remember a week or two into the school year when my 2 other roommates and I got back from a grocery run. We had just finished putting all the food away and I slowly closed the refrigerator, admiring the brightly glowing stacks of soda cans that filled at least 3 of the 5 shelves. I felt ridiculously powerful being in total control of my food. And full of sugar.

I remember watching junior and senior students draw. My mind exploded. I learned so much by just watching them. I picked up things in those first few weeks that I had never even thought of, techniques and materials that were new and amazing. When I used these tools and techniques myself I felt... like a rock star.

Our apartment was on the 12th floor. You could see for miles in every direction. It was in Detroit and every now and then we'd see smoke off in the distance. We'd grab our video camera and go chase it. Film whatever it was. Eat at White Castle. Drink more soda. It was bizarre and magical. It was classic art school.

I had always been a late night person. I didn't do mornings so much but could stay up late easily and plow into my creative work past 11, 12, 1, 2 or 3am without any trouble. This powerful creative rhythm was my time and apparently at art school, everyone embraced this rhythm. I finally felt like I was among my people. Time had no meaning, the floors in our apartment were constantly active and full of creative activity.

I remember one day I was about to take the stairs to go to class. A piece of paper was stuck to the door with a handwritten note in black marker. "Use at your own risk." Later I found out it was because someone had tried to take their own life and there was blood on the walls. They were fine but left the school after that. That was a moment that made me really think about the kinds of struggles that people could have so close to me.

I remember stopping on the highway to pick up car bumpers that had been torn off cars during collisions. We mounted these bumpers in our apartment. It was "art."

I remember microwaving all my meals and eating a ton of hot dogs. I remember on a whim buying some sort of blackened tuna patty thing in a box. And then microwaving it. That was the last time I bought a fish-related food item on purpose.

One time I bought a cheap new toilet at the hardware store. I decorated it with paint, fuzzy fabric, lights, and some glued-on accessories. We put it on a table in our room and it became quite the topic of conversation. I wish I could say that it lives on to this day but sadly my parents disposed of it after it sat in their basement for a decade. They said it was neither art nor a toilet. Oh well.

Somehow I survived. But here's the real point of the story. Even though car design had been my "one ultimate thing," after I got to the school and got a few months in I started to feel my world expand in a new way. I met so many people and had so many great experiences that something changed inside me. Or maybe not change, but evolve. I realized in the first semester something profound, something incredible.

God made me to be creative.

And I can be creative anywhere.

That's right, after going all the way, enrolling in quite possibly the best car design school in the country and sitting under the best teaching in industrial design that one could ever hope to learn from, I came to the realization that car design was not my thing.

Car design was not my thing? But it's always been my thing!

Everyone said it was my thing. I love drawing cars! I AM CAR DESIGN!

At first I was stunned. How could this be? Why was I feeling a disconnection to car design when I should be feeling a deeper and deeper connection? I'm here at art school fulfilling my destiny and pursuing the one thing that is so obviously my passion and calling. So why do I feel like I don't want to actually do this?

Sidenote: Here's the thing about being a car designer. It's elite. It's hard. There are more NBA players than car designers. You have to be both motivated and talented. You have to have that eye and that imagination but also technical execution and the chops to translate a vision into a sketch that people can understand. It's a very specific and demanding field. Now those things alone don't bother me; those aren't reasons not to pursue something. But the challenge ahead of me caused me to pause. "Is this what I want?" I didn't have a real clear answer to that question but after my first semester I knew that something inside me had changed. It was good. But also unnerving.

I recall walking into the school offices to inform the various staff that I would not be returning the next year. They were shocked to be honest (I don't think for this major that it happens very often). "You're not coming back? Why?" they asked me. I had trouble coming up with an answer. I felt like I should be returning, to finish what I started, to go all the way, to achieve my dream of becoming a car designer.

Except it wasn't my dream anymore.

I had a new sense of what "my thing" was. *It was being creative.* I could do anything, be creative anywhere... which sounds great, except for when it comes to telling your parents your plan. Because I had none.

SUMMARY: You may be the best in your school for something but you're probably not the best in the world. Or your state. Accept that.

BRAIN DUMP: If someone asked you what you're all about, what would you say? Do you have a sense of calling in your life? That there's a specific purpose or direction that it's your job to uncover?

Tips and advice for young creatives

Let's take a pause and talk about creativity and careers. If you're thinking about a career in something creative such as digital advertising, web, design, video or interactive media here is a list of some tips, advice, and resources to think about as you start to own more and more of your future. If you're looking at a career in something hyper-specific like automotive design or gaming then this can also apply. Basically, these are some rules of the road for ensuring you are on the right track to stand out from the competition and get to where you want to go. In no particular order, here are some "pro tips" for aspiring designers, marketers, filmmakers, communicators, and creatives:

Try Everything: Get experience in all different kinds of art forms and media. Don't get locked into one particular form like making logos, doing video or designing one thing. Try everything and get experience. You can tighten your focus later in your career.

Get Connected: Participate in forums and networks where you can share your work, get advice, have your work evaluated and get inspired. Make sure you take advantage of programs and offerings within your school system as well as extra-curricular activities.

Get Mentored: Find someone who's doing what you want to do one day. Talk to them, see where they work, how they do things. A little hands-on experience and job shadowing can go a long, long way.

Be Diverse: Start collecting your best work in all different kinds of art forms and media. Put together a portfolio that shows you are diverse and able to appreciate and work in many different types of design. Make sure you have a digital presence online and a simple way to point people to your online portfolio.

Save Your Work: Get organized and make sure you are saving all your work. Get in the habit of self-critiquing your work, constantly asking, "How could this be even better?" If you give away work to a friend or relative make sure you take good pictures of it before you give it away. Document all your work and keep a standing list of places your work has been used or displayed.

Take Some Risks: Opportunities come to those with initiative, not just people with talent. Just because you're good doesn't mean you'll automatically succeed. You have to have a marketable skill set as well as the confidence and initiative to go chase down what you want and pursue your goals. Talent is not enough.

Be Artsy, Be Organized: You've got to constantly grow and develop your skills as a creative person, that's a fact. But you also have to be a self-starter who is in control of your time and goals and able to organize your life, not just make amazing designs. There's nothing more frustrating than a great designer who is difficult to work with, unorganized, and a poor communicator. Be responsive, on-time, and polite, and your designs will be going places before you even show anyone your work.

Show Off: Take advantage of any opportunity to show your work; In school shows, at the local mall or bookstore, in your house, in your relative's houses, community centers, anywhere. All exposure is good but you have to be the one to initiate getting your work out there. Just go and ask.

Explore: Search for other artists and designers who are doing amazing work. Check out local shows and displays for inspiration. Get ideas and motivation from everywhere and everyone and always be analyzing and considering high-quality design work. Pick it apart. Reverse engineer it.

SUMMARY: Get organized about your work and think about how you do what you do a little bit more.

BRAIN DUMP: Which of the above two tips really jumped out to you? How can you take a step toward applying them right now?

I'm going to college again?!

Ok, back to art school. My Mom borrowed her boss's conversion van for the road trip back from Detroit to Maryland at the end of the spring semester. Not surprisingly I had acquired quite a bit of "art" during my first year including my fuzzy light-up toilet, various car bumpers, all the weird art school stuff you make in classes with names like "materials and processes" and "VisCom," and all my rock and roll gear (I was in a 2 man punk band. We were terrible.) Somehow we crammed it all in, I wedged myself in amongst the boxes of sketchbooks, odd-smelling hoodies, and disassembled desk parts, and we hit the road back to Maryland. Now I'm going to pause at this point and give some major shout-outs to my parents. They're self-admittedly not "artistic." They put up very well with my bizarre collections, room decorations, hardcore music, and decorated toilet art. I was an only child so maybe they just thought this was normal behavior but now, in retrospect, I can see that I was one weird kid. But hey, it's all good, my parents supported me in everything I did including bailing on the super elite art school after 1 year. And with no "what next."

It's a weird feeling.

Speaking of what next... what was next for me? What would you do? Imagine if the one thing that you are really good at, that all your friends and family mentioned about you whenever your name was brought up, and the one and only thing that you ever considered would be your future- imagine that no longer being "your thing." It can be terrifying. But also freeing. Right now I want you to pause and ask yourself this question:

If I didn't have that "one thing" that made me who I am... who would I be?

We'll come back to that later. And if you feel

like you don't have a "one thing" that's ok too. But let's get back to my life-after-art-school and tune in to what happens next.

When I was in high school my church youth group was always very important to me. At first my parents made me go and I had no choice in the matter but over time with the relationships, friends, and growth I experienced through a couple youth groups I attended, I really felt like the experience was essential in helping me become who I am today. As I was sitting there staring off into space wondering how to pick a future career and school path now having absolutely anything as a potential option I started to browse through Christian schools. I was browsing through programs offered at the Bible college closest to me in Maryland and suddenly a major jumped off the screen…. Youth Ministry.

Not everyone has eureka moments like this. I wish I could say that through a series of sophisticated questions and self-exploration that I was able to ascertain that youth ministry was the clear and obvious career path for someone like myself but, well, it wasn't like that at all. In fact, it was just one of those things that I felt like God showed me right there in that moment. Like magic. I know that's probably not helpful to you reading this book looking for some advice on finding the right major and school but let me unpack what I think led up to this moment. While you can't force a eureka moment to happen you can be ready to receive it. And this is how:

Be faithful: You have to be true to who you know yourself to be and have had some practice in separating what others want and expect from you and what you decide in your own heart is important. There's a second part too, the "faith" part of "faithful." You have to believe that your "what's next" will be revealed to you if your eyes are open and expectant. Have faith that the right door will be opened and be faith-ful to yourself and not simply what others desire for you. That's the first thing.

Be teachable: The worst thing in the world is someone who thinks they know everything and has it all figured out. Which is ironic because I'm sitting here writing a book that I'm sure is making the college and career finding thing look like a bunch of simple steps. Well, I hope that you're picking up here that it sure wasn't clear at the time and that I don't have it all figured out now. But in this step I encourage you to be teachable. Be confident in your choices and what you know but be open to the possibility that you don't know everything, you could be wrong, and there may be a smarter way to do things than what you already know. Even if this comes from your parents.

Be available: Have you heard the famous quote that half of life is just showing up? I believe this to be true but ultimately, showing up still isn't enough. You have to show up and be available. If you're someone that loves to plan and be in control then you have to be open to things not shaking out exactly as you planned. If you're someone that's more laid back and kind of lets life happen then you need to be available in a different way. You need to be ready to jump when God says jump. Regardless of your approach to life you have to not only show up but also be available for a new direction or change. Out of the blue. If you're faithful and you're teachable then you can be sure that this will always work out for the best, even if the path is a little windy.

I feel like at this moment of decision I was able to see this light bulb moment happen because I was faithful, teachable, and available. A lot of people didn't understand why I wasn't continuing on to pursue automotive design. They didn't get it. Especially when I told people that I was going to become a youth pastor and switch my educational track from slick-car-design to bible-theology-studying. It just didn't make sense. And I caught some heat from people that felt like this decision wasn't authentic to me and my calling. But I feel like if you make a real change in your life, if you make a decision that's going to count in the future for something, then it's going to come with some friction. Not everyone will see it. Not everyone will get it. Others will try to talk you out of it. You'll try to talk yourself out of it. You'll go back and forth a million times. There will be a thousand reasons to consider.

But you'll know. I eventually did. Once I took a few steps that direction.

Here's how the rest of this story takes shape: I looked at the programs, knew that the youth ministry track was what I wanted, drove down to the school for a tour, filled out some papers, and in just a few weeks was setting foot on campus as a Freshman. Again. On one hand it was a bit disappointing that I was starting over again completely from scratch (ok, I did transfer a couple fine art credits). On the other hand I think my parents were really excited to pay substantially less per semester at this small Bible college rather than my ridiculously expensive elite art school. But hey, it's just money!

I started the program knowing no one at this school. Again.

I began all the basic classes from scratch. Again.

I didn't know if I would find any close friends at this school, especially since the bulk of the students were commuters. But I did. In fact, tons of the people I met at school this first year I am still in touch with today.

Here are my top memories from Bible College:

I remember starting a "gang" called the Back Row Thugs (BRT). Our big thing was that we would park in the back row of the parking lot and turn our wheels left. Why? Just to have a thing. We even had membership cards. I even got them laminated. We were also a men's accountability group who got together weekly to encourage each other and do manly stuff like go to Taco Bell.

I remember when I really got to see how the original languages of the Bible worked and where they came from. The fact that the ancient texts were available, readable, and not that different from modern versions of Greek and Hebrew blew my mind. While I did terribly in my Koine Greek classes I did learn enough to be able to stumble my way through the text, grasp aspects of the original languages unique to the time, and be able to generate small group discussion questions to really help people grow.

I met my wife at college. In Principles of Biblical Interpretation. I thought she was vegan. She wasn't. On one of our first dates I watched her eat an entire rack of ribs with fries. I'm married to her now.

I remember chapel services and having guest speakers come in all the time. This was great getting to hear so many different perspectives and experiences within the broader Christian story. I loved that we had guest speakers in who made us nervous, who were not from our particular backgrounds.

The college I went to was the most ethnically diverse Bible college in the nation. It was a blend of every possible ethnic group you might encounter in the Washington DC region. I had classes with students of every age, ethnic group, income range, and life experience. I didn't really appreciate this until after I graduated and realized just how much this opened up my perspective.

I graduated, even with my less-than-optimal grades in Koine Greek. I look back on these times with fond memories and the friends I made then I continue to have today.

SUMMARY: Only you can know your next steps. Not everyone will get it and a little friction lets you know you're taking a risk.

BRAIN DUMP: Was there ever a time where you felt like a decision suddenly became clear to you? Like a revelation or an epiphany? What was it like?

How to get an internship

Internships are huge. And not just to check the box for college credit. Whenever and however you can, you should take internships. There are two basic reasons why you should prioritize this over just about everything else. First is that you will have an easier time getting your foot in the door at a powerhouse agency or company as an intern than trying to apply as a brand-new graduate to their workforce. So forget about what they'll pay and just get yourself in the front door. And once you're in the door, learn all you can and soak everything up. It doesn't matter what the scope of your internship is, once you're inside and you feel the rhythm of the environment you will start to see all the opportunities you have there to learn, shadow, and experience on a level you otherwise couldn't. Employers of high performing workplaces are most often very open to internship programs, especially if they're not too demanding on their leadership and are from an affiliate with an emotional connection like a school or church.

Now, the second benefit: relationships. The most important thing for you to get out of your internship are relationships. Even though you may be the lowest person on the totem pole you will suddenly have access to people who are doing amazing things in their careers, can open doors for you, help you in ways you can't imagine, and connect you with other organizations and people down the road when the time is right for you to pursue something specific. If you're motivated, a self-starter, have a good attitude, and are ready to work on anything that comes your way, you will be poised to build some very important relationships with people in that organization. I've seen and heard this happen on countless occasions and have been on the other side as well, where I've been able to support and help interns beyond the scope of what they were there to do at our place of business, and connect them with people or resources down the road to help them accelerate their goals.

Now on to the "how." Let's say you're considering an internship as part of a college requirement or maybe for a summer break. There are probably 5,000 other students considering the same thing at the same kinds of places. So how do you increase your odds of getting a conversation with someone at the kind of place where you'd like to intern? Here are some secret tips that not everyone else will think of:

1. Be (almost) annoying. A mistake that a lot of intern seekers make is only inquiring about an internship one time and then accepting whatever answer they're given (if they even get through to someone). This is a gigantic missed opportunity. You should reach out to every organization on your list at least 5 times before you cross them off your list. There are a lot of reasons for doing this and trust me, you won't be annoying. It will be seen as initiative. And it increases your odds. Sometimes organizations aren't ready for an intern yet. Others don't have a

point of contact in their company to handle it. Other times the voicemail you left gets deleted. Your email gets caught in the spam folder. Even if you get to someone and they say "no" it's not over yet. Many interns who are offered positions at a company end up choosing something else at the last minute leaving that position at the first company back on the table. There are countless reasons to reach out repeatedly so make sure you do.

2. Look to your parents and friends. The worst thing you can do when seeking an internship is to go to your school's list of employers who are looking for interns and simply end your search there. Everyone else will do that. And what if no one on that list really gets you excited or is the right industry for you? Check the list. Send in your application. But now it's time to rely on the *real* method of making it happen which is looking to the relationships your parents (and their friends) have in the business community. I know it's a little humbling to go to your parents asking for help

but trust me on this one. Tell your parents about your internship need. Ask them who they know. If they're on social media, look at who they're connected with. Ask them to ask their friends. You're always just one or two connections away from the right person who can get you an introduction at the place you really want to intern.

3. Alumni network. Something that's often overlooked by students is tapping into the power of their school's alumni network. What's that you ask? Basically, after you graduate, your school will continue to communicate with you, usually to ask you for money since most colleges and universities constantly need donations to keep running, and to try to keep graduates connected as they spill out from the school's region and into the global workforce. Although you may not be a graduate now, trust me, once you graduate you will have an eternal connection with other people from your school, and it will be a powerful one. Friends help out friends. Alumni help out alumni. Family helps out family.

And something that very successful people like to do in business is help out the schools they graduated from, both financially and with things like helping interns get placed. So the best thing you can do is find and reach out to your school's alumni coordinator. Tell them your need and they'll look at everyone they know to try to help. It's not a guarantee but it's a huge leg up on the competition.

4. Make up your own internship. This last tip is a big one and requires some guts on your part. Essentially, if you know of a place that you'd like to intern, you've checked their website and found that they have no current openings, you should still try to get a conversation going with them and make up your own internship just for you. It sounds ridiculous, right? Just reach out to someone you don't know at a company that seems pretty amazing to make a case for a position that doesn't exist, just so you can have an internship? Yes. Exactly. This is hustle at its finest. Find the right person, do your 5 calls and emails, and then if nothing else

works, walk in the front door every day for a week until you're sitting in someone's office talking about why you want this so bad. Of all the things business leaders juggle all day long, this is actually the least of their drama. You're not a pest, you're being proactive. Show the initiative. Push hard. Be polite, offer what you can, and then wait. Try this process enough times and you will soon see that most of the unspoken rules of how things happen in life are kind of made up.

Well, that's about all my secret sauce on how to get an internship. Here are a few other final parting words on the topic:

- Even if a position is filled, if you can get a person on the phone, ask them if they'd consider another intern as well for the same position. For free.
- Never start a conversation with how much the internship pays. It's not about you making money, it's about you getting huge doses of real world experience.

- If you see something you want to learn or participate in at the place you're interning, just ask if you can shadow or be involved. The answer will almost always be yes.
- If you can eat lunch with people who are doing what you want to do one day, do it.
- Ask questions. Constantly. Try everything.
- Forget what your agreement says about the internship's end date. If you're loving it and providing value to the organization you can always have the discussion about extending your internship down the road.
- Many interns often come back or stick around and become full time employees. So don't focus on your end date.
- Don't burn bridges. Stay positive, learn all you can, and if for some reason things don't go well, don't make any permanent bad decisions there. End on a high note and move on. You'll be glad you did.
- Update your resumé. Your internship experience is incredibly valuable as someone just starting out in their career. Focus on the problems you helped solve during your internship and less on the tasks you did all

day. If you did something to save the company money or helped them make more, then definitely add that information in.

In the next chapter we'll talk about how one of my internships turned out to be a career move in disguise.

SUMMARY: Pursue internships based on your own rules, not just what you see posted on a website.

BRAIN DUMP: Where would you ideally like to intern? Is there a specific place/organization or is it more for a certain kind of work? From the above list of tips, which two jump out to you the most as things you can start taking action on or pursuing in order to score the best internship possible?

I'm in ministry?

Growing up I was a military kid until my Dad semi-retired and we stayed in one place for a long time. I was born in Germany and we had stints living in Philadelphia, California, Kansas, and probably other places that I'm not recalling. As a kid I thought everyone drank black coffee and had cold meat sandwiches for breakfast. I thought that traveling in a cold, windowless cargo jet, facing backward, wearing earplugs, and drinking water from a Gatorade cooler lashed to a metal pole was just how everyone flew. I didn't realize that flying military "Space A" in the top section of a C-5A Galaxy Ranger was actually pretty weird. But as a military kid with no siblings this is just the kind of flexibility and go-with-the-flow mentality I had to have.

Fast forward to living in Maryland and realizing that my experiences in military air travel were actually NOT experiences that all my friends could relate to, I found myself growing up in a picturesque chunk of suburbia with good friends and schools and at a solid church in the area. During my youth group and college days I started to ask more questions about life and faith and attending a Presbyterian church there was certainly a lot of emphasis on rational discourse on all things faith. As I came into my senior year at Bible college I needed an internship, one thing led to another and I soon found myself graduated and working full time at my home church overseeing middle school and high school youth group programs.

It was a really good gig. They even gave me a credit card. A credit card! Can you believe it? I had an office with a legitimate desk lamp and a whiteboard. It was great. During these years as an intern-turned-youth-director I learned a ton. And had a lot of fun. Being young at heart and not too far away from the teen years myself, youth pastoring was a great fit for me and I think my wife and I were able to help a lot of students with the ups and downs of the teen years. Here's just a few things I remember:

We needed a name for our spring retreat. We jokingly made a flyer with a picture of a folding chair on it. The name stuck, it became tradition, and The Chair retreat was born. Completely stupid? Yes. A memorable experience for all? Definitely.

Speaking of chairs I recall building an 8-foot tall one out of plywood in the church parking lot. It eventually fell over. I don't know where it is now.

I remember a pie-eating contest. Hay bale mazes. Fundraisers. A trip to Japan. Coffee houses. Music. Student leadership teams. Taking students out to talk. Tackling some really tough questions about life and faith. Tackling even harder conversations with parents and their students. It was fun. It was hard. I was used by God to play a specific role in students' lives- a role where I wasn't their parent and wasn't their friend. But I could be a person of influence in their lives and point them to God, a rare position to be in.

Years passed. My wife and I had our first baby. I had never changed a diaper before that. Once. In my life. Hey, I was an only child, don't judge me. Long story short. I felt that my most rewarding memories during this time were when I was putting together experiences. Making teaching memorable. Organizing events and activities that really sent a message, that immersed students in what we were talking about. One time we were doing a special night on the persecuted church and I set up an entire experience out in the field behind our church at night. No one was allowed to talk. Silently we went out into the field to read stories, see pictures, and contemplate what was happening to our brothers and sisters throughout the world, many of whom experience significant hardships and direct persecution because of the fact that they are Christians. I remember putting together a lot of these types of experiences and really enjoyed it.

The takeaway? *Creative communication.* That was the common thread. It felt the same as when I was in art school. The difference was that instead of drawing cars and rendering objects I was teaching the Bible and creating experiences. But both of these things felt the same to me. When I was really in my element, doing my thing, forgetting about times and costs and just chasing a creative vision in my mind, this was what fueled me. This was what got me going. This is where I was able to make a real impact.

Looking back I was really fortunate to have a church that would give me so much leeway and freedom to do whatever I wanted (except they never let me buy that motorcycle for the ministry). And as the years passed I continued to pursue doing more and more creative things at church and helping students and teams capture what God was trying to teach them.

Near the end of my time at church I had a feeling that I was detaching. It's hard to explain. It's not that anything was going bad or that I suddenly didn't care about ministry anymore, it's just that I had that feeling of "graduating out," of moving on. Like I was on my senior year of this job and something big and different was coming next. Can you relate?

I was doing more and more video at the time and thought that my next professional adventure might be doing something exclusively focused on video. My good friend from art school and I talked about partnering up to launch a new video company. Or offer a variety of creative services, like a creative agency. I even met with an accountant. I crunched numbers (not my thing just so you know). What happened next? I decided I would head out solo and launch my own design and creative services business. I concluded my time as a youth pastor, had an awesome farewell dinner, packed up my 6,000 pounds of books and weird decorations from my office (not the fuzzy toilet), and set out to pursue this vision on my own. Well, as anyone who has been down this road will tell you, you never really succeed alone. The support of my wife, clients, and friends was vital to help me get up and running and in a few chapters I'll tell you why you should NEVER run your own company. Or why you should DEFINITELY run your own company. You read it and decide.

SUMMARY: When you have a strong feeling that you are detaching from something in your life, listen to it but don't make any rash decisions. Get counsel. Don't ignore the feeling and always work to savor the things in your current context that are really fulfilling to how you live and work.

BRAIN DUMP: Have you ever had the feeling of detaching from something? What was it like? Do you have that feeling about anything in your life right now?

How to think about your "personal brand"

Here's a question for you. For whatever your degree is in, how many other people in your region are graduating with the same degree? Now another question. For all the people graduating with that degree, how are you different from them? This is the heart and soul of thinking about your "personal brand." Branding is a bit of a buzz word right now but didn't use to be part of our everyday speech. Branding and "brands" are obviously connected so let's start there. What makes a "brand"? Is it their logo? The colors they use? Whether their website imagery comes across as very serious or playful? Well, to some degree it's all of these things but all of them combined.

I've heard "brand" describe as simply "the story that surrounds the company." I like this way of describing it for two reasons. First, a brand is not merely the visual appearance it conveys through its website or advertising. It also cannot be conveyed in one image or logo. Second, a story is something that can't be communicated instantly, it's something that you experience over time. You add more elements to the story each time you encounter that particular organization. So let's run with the "story that surrounds you" idea and talk a little bit about why you need to think about yourself as a brand and then drill down into what your brand is about.

As you may have picked up by now I believe very strongly that you need to take ownership over your own career path, education, and experience. How you approach defining your personal brand is simply part of that ownership and a powerful decision-making tool you'll use yourself but that will also impact how others perceive you. Ok, I understand that this sounds a little wishy washy. Let me break it down like this:

What personal branding is not

- It's not a list of how amazing you are

- It's not a logo that represents you
- It's not your resumé
- It's not your portfolio or collection of work

What personal branding is

- It is a series of statements that explains how you are unique
- It is a series of statements that communicates who you are
- It is a series of statements that tells others what's important to you
- It is a unified way to tell others about your portfolio, resumé, and experiences
- It is a way to distinguish yourself when talking to an employer
- It is words, images, emotions, and the sum of all their parts

If you're a visual person or someone who loves graphics or design then you may already be thinking miles down the road about how you'll visually communicate the essence of your personal brand. But slow down tiger, let's do some groundwork first before we start slinging pixels and picking fonts. From the above list you can see that I've used the word "statements" a lot of times. That's because the most fundamental step in defining your brand is to distill down who you are into a series of specific, and carefully chosen words. Impossible right? Maybe. The benefit is that you are forcing yourself to take something huge and expansive (like your soul) and attempt to boil it down to the words and phrases that best describe your uniqueness. It's not a natural thing. But let's try it together and then we can get to some of the fun stuff about branding. Here are some questions to get your mind going in the right direction:

- If I could pick 3 words that best describe me I would pick:
- 3 words that other people use to describe me are:
- Something that's often said about me is that I'm the person that always:
- My favorite quote is:
- My favorite book is:
- The reason it's my favorite book is because (only use 1 sentence):
- When I get together with my friends it's very important to me that we:
- My favorite thing to do when I'm alone

and have some time to myself is to:

- My teachers often describe me as:
- Over my entire life the 3 accomplishments I'm most proud of are:
- If I had to write out what I think my mission in life is I would say:
- 3 activities that I love to do are:
- My favorite subjects in school have been:
- A hero of mine, either real or fictional is:
- The activity that makes me feel the greatest sense of satisfaction is:
- If I had to pick one thing in my life that probably hasn't happened to anyone else I know it is:

Whew, that's a lot of deep questions. How did you do? You probably had a couple of these questions that stumped you, that got you stuck. That's ok. The goal isn't to fill out this list like you're applying for a job, it's to get your mind into the habit of taking an abstract topic and boiling it down into a single sentence or group of words. It doesn't come easy to everyone so if you're having trouble just make some notes (yes, you can write in this book), and keep moving. We'll come back to this later. Now here's the next set of fill-in-the-blanks I want you to go through:

- My name is (your name)
- I've been told that I'm (list 3 traits)
- I see myself as a (future job title) who always (describe how you like to work)
- I feel that I am very unique as a (future job) because (describe 2 reasons)
- I love to (activity) because when I do I feel (describe feeling)
- It's important to me to always (phrase that describes how you relate to others)
- Looking back, I have a few accomplishments I'm extremely proud of. They are (list a few)
- I feel like through all of them the common link between them was (describe what they all had in common).
- This is something important to me that I carry with me into my next career as a (future job title)

How did this go for you? Did you have any moments of clarity? Any surprises? Where did you get stuck? This exercise is meant to force you into describing feelings with words and finding common aspects of your past that can describe how you see yourself in the future. It may not be perfect or complete but it's a starting place for you to think about how you're unique to everyone else professionally and how to put into words all the awesome ways that you are you. Now that we've done some of this basic past/present work, let's see how we might translate some of these words and concepts into something you could use for your portfolio, resumé, or school application.

Portfolio

A way to think about your portfolio is to focus on a common story throughout all your work. In the above section you may have identified a few key themes that you could use to give a name to your portfolio website or to describe your work. From here you can define a color palette for your personal brand and maybe even a logo. And remember, a logo doesn't have to be a major project. A simple typeface with the right colors can communicate a lot. For example, if you identified that you are someone who brings people together and that it's important for you to include everyone in a group and have fun together then you could look for a font where the letters all connect to each other. Or a font that's more fun or lively. If you're working on your personal website or logo then you could think of images that show things connecting. Maybe it's puzzle pieces or rope tied together. Maybe it's a woven bracelet or tapestry. These are all ways that you can translate your personal brand essence (in this example, "connections") into words, type, and images.

Resumé

A way to make your resumé stand out is to have a great cover letter that tells a potential employer how you're unique or different and communicates a compelling reason why you would be a great fit for their organization. You'll hear a lot of different opinions on cover letters but let's just say that you are going to submit your resumé with a cover letter and that it has to really be good. Ok, so we're not going to discuss everything about resumés here but what we can think about is finding a common story that links your past education, activities, and interests all together. If we go back to the "connecting people" idea in our example above then we could use that as part of our introduction letter. We could also use that to describe our specific role in extra curricular activities. In terms of work we could show how we connected the dots to solve problems or connected groups of people to get things done. You get the idea. It may work, it may not, all I'm saying is that if you have a sense of what your story is then you can use that to stand out from everyone else.

School / scholarship application

If you're applying to college, a college transfer, or graduate school, then chances are you're going to be doing some writing for the application process. This is a great opportunity to put your personal brand to the test and do some persuasive writing that fleshes out those elements of you that you identified above. Most applications to schools will require some writing so this is your chance to tell your story. Look at the above lists and see if any of those could serve as story starters for your essay. Maybe you can build on one of those questions and explain how you arrived at your personal brand. Perhaps the question is on something very specific but you're not sure how to give an answer that's unique to you. Use your personal brand.

That's your perspective, your unique platform. No one else has that. Whether it's a school application, an essay contest, scholarship, or blog post, your personal brand is a tool in your toolbox that you can use to define your unique voice, personality, and perspective. Use it.

Oh, and before we forget. The fun stuff. Yes, do the fun stuff. Make a cool logo for yourself. Build your personal website or portfolio site. Make a YouTube channel and create some videos if you're into that. But make sure you do the hard work first to unearth the stories and words that best describe you and your place in the universe, then you can add the sparkle.

SUMMARY: Your personal brand is the story of you.

BRAIN DUMP: Can you summarize your personal brand in one sentence? Try it! From the list of questions and fill-in-the-blanks, which two or three really stood out to you? Why? What is one practical step you can take in your own life from this chapter?

I'm starting my own business?!

You know what's really stressful? Having no predictable source of income in your life.

Now I know this sounds like a serious grown-up problem, let me put it to you this way. Imagine all the cool things in your life. Now imagine how much all those cool things cost. Now imagine suddenly you need to pay for all those things without your parents. Tomorrow. Scary?

Now imagine having a baby and a mortgage.

By this time in my life I was full-on into my adult years. There's never really a great time to start your own business, something I knew, but you never realize how much you depend on the stability of your life until major parts of it are no longer stable. With a slight plan, a brand-new MacBook and a lot of motivation, I set out to launch my new company serving clients with graphic design, social media strategies, web design, video production, and creative communication consulting. A few things I recall from this time:

There are few endeavors as exciting as dreaming about what your own brand can be. You have total freedom and control to define your unique place in the world with what you do. It's incredible and is one of the boldest creative acts you can take.

Doing your own thing means disciplining your own life in a way you never thought possible. With no external factors influencing how you will spend your days you will need to take charge of your greatest asset, your time, and summon the discipline needed to give all your time a job.

Taxes. I told my accountant I could only meet with him for one hour at a time because I literally would get a headache after more than that. Numbers. Laws. Rules. Exemptions. If you can hire someone to do this stuff then do it. If you're gifted this way then even better. And if you have an accountant make sure you take care of them. I still get chills thinking about filing my yearly corporate taxes. Ironically, by the time I was done doing my own thing I finally understood enough of the tax system to do it correctly. Go figure.

I remember when a client's website was hacked and I stayed up most of the night attempting to fix it, having no idea what to do, and feeling pretty alone and hopeless. I assume it was eventually resolved (I've erased this memory) but this was a dark day.

I remember committing to a multi-month net-working sponsorship opportunity and having my booth set up right alongside some big players in our region. It was awesome to feel like my little outfit was right there as an equal player alongside some of the biggest brands in the area. Granted, I had a fraction of the resources and none of the money but I learned how to attract a crowd and work a room. These skills have paid off tremendously.

I remember the feeling of winning business and receiving checks. There are few things like it. You, having nothing but your passion and portfolio, meet a potential client, hear what they need, pitch them a proposal, they agree, you do work, and then they pay you real money. It's incredible.

Feast or famine. This is often the name of the game when you run your own company. Some months you receive a truckload of payments and all of a sudden you're thinking about buying another car "just for fun." The next month you are trying to think of creative ways to buy ground meat. And growing whatever else you need to eat in your backyard garden. Ok, I'm exaggerating a little bit here but listen to me here, running your own business is great. But it's hard. You'll learn a ton though and have a perspective that it's simply impossible to have unless you've done it. The trick is to do this kind of thing soon. While you're young. While you have some margin to fail. While you can learn financial lessons the hard way when it's just you and you can crash on a friend's couch and eat their Ramen noodles for a few weeks. When you have a house and a family it's a different ballgame.

I don't say any of this to discourage you from entrepreneurship.

In fact, quite the opposite. Do your own thing.

Always be running your own side thing. Have side work and side clients and expand your network and build your personal brand. Do it. But do it early and learn fast. Even if you decide that running your own company isn't really your passion, you'll learn so much by doing your own thing that you'll be even more valuable in the future as you work for other organizations and people.

During this time I remember God answering prayers with checks in the mail. I remember having some hard conversations with clients about how I messed up a project or how they were wrong or how they just didn't like my creative work. I learned that it's really hard to not identify yourself with your work and not take it personally when your creative work is criticized. I also learned that you should be extremely thankful to have the opportunities to develop your own business and have freedom to do your own thing. This is a unique blessing and an enormous chunk of the world's population does not have access to the same opportunities and structures that would allow them to be entrepreneurs as easily.

If you can do your own thing, do it. And enjoy

the ride.

SUMMARY: Entrepreneurship will teach you a ton. Start your own thing while you're young and fail fast and often. Learn constantly and always have something you're doing on the side.

BRAIN DUMP: If you had to start your own company or go freelance right now, what would you do?

How to start your side gig overnight

Entrepreneurship. Big word. A lot of letters. When we hear of it we think of Steve Jobs or Elon Musk or the countless leaders of social media or tech startups like Snapchat, Facebook, or Uber. But can I share a little secret with you? Entrepreneurship is so much bigger than this. It's not a "thing" that billionaires or tech startups do. It's a mindset, a way of thinking, a process of starting things that anyone from any industry can embrace. I like to think of entrepreneurship as simply a way of taking ownership over things you care about in your life and pushing them ahead in creative ways with a certain goal in mind. In this chapter I want to talk specifically about entrepreneurship as it relates to your "side gig."

Throughout this book we've talked about doing your own thing, having your own "side hustle" and being in the habit of developing your skills and portfolio outside of your classes, program, or day job. So what I want to do now is walk through a process of how you could develop, launch, and accelerate a side business or service overnight. If you're reading this book then I assume you have some interest or openness to a career in creative work but I think the below can apply to anyone, regardless of what career path you may be considering.

Phase 1: Plan Your What

Decide what you're selling

The first thing to do when it comes to your side gig is to figure out what you're selling. Essentially, ask yourself what you can do that's in demand in your area that you know how to do. Bonus if it's something you've done many, many times. Maybe it's web design, video creation, lawn mowing, cat video GIF-making, or graphic design. In this first step identify the goods or services that you're going to offer. Try to be specific and don't pick too many things.

Outline your network

Oftentimes it's not enough to simply identify what you can do. What if no one wants it? This step in the process is your chance to identify who exactly you're going to target. You may find that the people you're targeting have a specific need in one area. Or there may be a lot of competition and you should pick something else. In this step, list who you're going to approach with your service. You don't have to know names, just list companies, roles, people, or industries.

Determine the value

You have to set some prices. Chances are you'll sell yourself too cheap if you're young. It's one of the biggest mistakes I've seen younger entrepreneurs make, charging too little for their services. You may think that a low price increases your chances of getting hired but not everyone considers the price the main factor in deciding who to hire. Oftentimes business people will select the more expensive firm or freelancer because their higher price communicates their professional value. Cheaper isn't always better. Oh, one more thing. If you're going to talk the talk...

Phase 2: Look Ahead

Craft the story

Now you're going to put some of these elements together and attempt to write a paragraph about what you're selling, who you're selling it to, and how much it costs. This is the heart and soul of promoting your side gig so it's important here to be as specific as possible. Remember, it's just as important to identify what you're NOT going to do and who you're NOT going to reach as it is the other way around. This narrowness will help you focus faster.

Set your goals

Once you have these basics figured out you can set a goal related to your side gig. It might be a financial goal, like making $1000 during X period of time. Or perhaps you have a different goal such as building 5 business websites over the summer for your portfolio. No matter what your target may be it's important to define it as clearly as possible and to set a goal number with an end date. There's a saying about scoreboards. Without one, there's no game.

Speak to the objections

Here's where you'll get some practice in the secret sauce of selling. Your next step in establishing your side hustle is to actually go out and start talking to people but before you, do, it's time to nail down some responses to the objections you'll probably hear. Regardless of what your selling you'll typically encounter the same 3 objections or "no thanks" reasons. What do you think those objections are for your business? It might be "It's too expensive," or "I don't really need that," or maybe even, "Not right now." Think about how to answer these objections so that you're ready when people might say them.

Phase 3: Make Stuff

Package it up

Time for the fun stuff. By now you've laid the groundwork with the basics of what you're offering, how much it costs, and how to talk about your offer to your audience. Now it's time to make some cool stuff to promote it. Maybe it's a website, emails, graphics, logo, print flyers, etc. This kind of thing may come easily to you or it might be more of a challenge. The key here is not to get bogged down pursuing perfection in your promotional work or to attempt creating a museum worth of designs. Pick the 3 most important things you need to promote your services and make a first draft of all of them. This will ensure you don't lose momentum in the process.

Outline the ecosystem

You now know what you're selling and to whom. You have the tools to reach your audience and you know how to talk about your services. Your next step in the process is to create a marketing ecosystem. An ecosystem is just a fancy term for outlining all the steps in how you'll reach out to your audience, promote your service, follow up, follow up again, and get paid. Remember, people usually have to hear about you and your service at least 7 times before they respond. If you already have a relationship with your audience then the likelihood of a positive response early on increases with less touches.

Pick your push and pull

Most of your early days with your business will be pushing. No one is going to come find you for your service, it's up to you to go out there and knock on doors (literally or figuratively). So stop assuming that anyone's going to discover your slick 1 page website at all and instead, push people to it. The greater the personal style of connection, the better your chances. In other words, the most effective methods for getting people to buy your services are (most to least effective): Face-to-face meetings, phone calls, personal emails (not a group blast), snail mail letters, text messages, group emails.

Is that too many steps? Maybe. Is it the basic list of how you can take nothing but an idea and transform it into a viable business overnight? Yes, it is. No one said it will be easy. No one's even saying that it's going to turn you a profit. But go through the process, develop yourself as you go, and you'll see results.

What's the worst that could happen?

SUMMARY: The more times you start a side gig, the better you'll get at doing it. And you can build on a process that works.

BRAIN DUMP: If you had to start a new side gig this weekend what would it be? List a few other side gigs you could possibly do this summer or in the next three months. From the list of launch tasks, which two most excite you? Which two seem the most daunting or challenging?

I'm going to work at a law firm?!

Question: What's a word that's more important than it is trendy?

Answer: Stability.

After running my business for almost two years I could feel the need for more stability in our family's life. This need for stability was mostly in two areas, finances and time. Finances in the sense that it isn't very easy to have unpredictable margin in your money and not have steady income coming in. And with time it's very hard to work constantly. When you work from home there is always the temptation to be working all the time, to lose the ability to turn off. I experienced both these things and as we started to think about having more children and having my wife change jobs, the need for stability become a very high priority.

Now don't get me wrong. I loved doing what I was doing. It was a rush. I got to be creative, do my own thing, set my own schedule, and be my own boss. At 20-something years of age this is a big deal and as I concluded my Master's Degree (I forgot to mention that I got a Master's somewhere during this insane timeframe), the need to change my work to something more predictable became obvious. This wasn't the easiest thing to do. It's the same challenge as getting your business running when you have a regular full time job. At what point do you have enough margin, enough time to go ahead and make the leap? When are you in a good position to make the jump to your what's next?

The answer? You're never ready.

There's never a time where all the stars are aligned for you to seamlessly make a jump from one thing to another, from working for someone else to working for yourself, from working for yourself to transitioning to working for someone else. So let's get that out of the way. But there's a sweet spot. If you're paying attention and have some good counsel in your life you'll know when the time is right. But you'll never just saunter over from one thing to the other without a crunch, without a little friction, without a little chaos. This is ok. That friction is what's letting you know that you're investing yourself into what you do all day. The trick is to surround yourself with people that have been where you've been before, that are smart, wise, and that know you and what you're about enough to be able to warn or encourage you. If you're doing this and you're not running *from* something but running *to* something, you'll land just fine. Don't worry.

The way it happened for me was pretty interesting. As I met with my current clients to see what other work I could do for them I soon found myself in front of one of my clients, a law firm, and quickly sensed their need for a full time person for their creative services. While I had enjoyed doing some work for them in the past, it wasn't actually legal in nature. I was doing posters and websites and signage and logos, all fun creative stuff that mostly demanded I copy and paste any "legalese" from one of their emails or a document. Actually, I imagined working at a law firm would be something quite different.

One thing led to another and it became clear that this might be a great opportunity for me. The location was good, the people were cool, and the pay was stable. I took the job. Here are a few stand-out moments I remember from being the "super creative guy" at a legal and regulatory consulting and law firm:

On my first day I wore a tie. Then I had to build my own office chair. I was tucked in the far back corner of a small office space because the firm was growing in people but adapting their small space. I didn't care. I was getting paid.

I learned about how search engine optimization works. It was the first time I really saw how left brained analysis and rationality could pair with right-brained creativity and visuals. It's a skillset that's become really valuable to me over the years but not something I thought I'd ever learn.

I remember messing up a website form pretty bad and not immediately fixing it. It was bad. I felt bad. That was a bad day. Obviously not the end of the world but I felt like I let my bosses down and I could have easily avoided it. Everyone has a memory like this at their current job or at school so that's ok. This feeling has taught me to learn to better discipline my own emotions and to be able to accept the fact that I will make mistakes in my work.

I remember talking the leadership into a ridiculous marketing scheme involving a fake product, stuffed unicorns, and a very expensive trade show booth for a large natural products event. They went for it. It was a runaway success. I felt awesome to have come up with it and to see it become a reality. To this day people still talk about it.

I had to learn the actual law. The real, United States, law. The Food Safety Modernization Act. HACCP. Warning letters. Compliance. I learned how to read legalese and even how to write a little bit of it. I still use some of these writing skills but now for practical jokes. I'm thankful now that I was pushed to learn this "foreign language" but at the time it hurt my brain cells. A lot.

In a smaller organization you become close with the people you work with. Like a second family. Maybe it's because just like in a real family, everyone has to pull their weight, wear a bunch of different hats, and do whatever it takes to get the job done. We moved offices. Had an office Olympics. Celebrated birthdays. Experienced the pain of loss. Got mad. Made up. Did awesome things together. This is all part of the experience and no matter what your family background, working with people professionally will oftentimes feel a lot like being part of a family. You should savor these times.

Looking back on my time at the law firm I have very positive memories. Granted, it was not your normal law office but more like a hip startup that happened to do mind-crushing legal and regulatory compliance work, BUT I learned so much during this time. But let's recap my life so far:

- Went to automotive design school
- Went to Bible college
- Became a youth pastor
- Got married. Bought a house. Had a baby.
- Started and ran a creative company
- Got a Master's Degree
- Went to work for a law firm

This doesn't make sense. Right? If you look at

the above and try to connect the dots it really looks like someone copy and pasted excerpts from 5 different people's resumés and stuck them all together. It's not cohesive. It seems disconnected. It seems spastic. Yet I love that this is my story and the path that God led me through. Looking back it's clear that this actually is a very cohesive story. The pathway does make sense. There is a common thread and natural evolution from one thing to the next. It's in the title of this book and it's my story in a nutshell. It's my creative thread. See it?

In the coming pages I'm going to talk a little bit about the next chapters in my story. I'm going to talk about going all-in at an ad agency, how I became a YouTube celebrity, what I'm doing now, and how I see the pieces falling together and connecting when it comes to my family and kids (now I have 4 boys, wow!)

SUMMARY: Don't write off a potential career choice because of what you think it will be like. And remember, the same type of work or industry could be very different depending on what you do in it and who you actually work for.

BRAIN DUMP: Is there anything you've been a part

of in your past that at the time didn't make sense but now is obvious how it was the perfect thing for you? Are there any decisions you're faced with in your life right now where you are struggling to make a choice and not sure what to do? Name 3 people in your life who you could look to or meet with for counsel, wisdom, and advice.

Let's talk about you

Wow, are you still reading my book at this point? Congrats! Hopefully by now you've seen that while you may not have a precise sense of direction about your future career path or education you can have confidence that you'll land well with each milestone in your life if you have your head up and your eyes open. Throughout my story you probably read a few things that seemed like advice. Well, it's true. In addition to sharing my own story I'd like to give you some advice. Stuff I wish I knew back when I was graduating high school or in college. Things that I know now that I just didn't back then. I'm giving you some direct advice not because I know it all but because I think if you read this far in my book, you're ready to take some action yourself.

So maybe you're wondering... why entrepreneurship?

If you were so excited to read this book that you missed the extra words on the cover that said "entrepreneurship," let me connect the dots so that the next chunk of pages make sense. In my story you've hopefully noticed a few common elements when I shared about the soul searching and brain pains of each major career move in my life. At the heart of each those changes was not simply "thinking it through" or writing down "pros" and "cons" on a piece of paper. To me, what really helped me make strong transitions between things that otherwise may not seem like they connect, was having a deeply ingrained sense of self-ownership. For this book we're going to just use "self-ownership" and "self-starting" and "entrepreneurship" synonymously. But in case all you're thinking about is whether or not this book is going to help you launch the next Tesla, here's what I'm defining as the key ingredients to having an entrepreneurial mindset. Thankfully, they make a pretty memorable acronym, "P.R.O."

Perseverance.

If you're someone that's had to fight for things before, or had struggles in your life that you fought to overcome, then you'll be familiar with perseverance. I use it here as a key ingredient to entrepreneurship because so much of starting, launching, and creating involves battling and struggling and pushing through to an extraordinary result. Sometimes the battle is against the unknown, a lack of knowledge. Sometimes the battle is against our own fears. Other times, the struggle can be interpersonal. However the struggle takes shape, having an entrepreneurial mindset means anticipating the challenge and fighting through it.

Reinvention.

I love the word "reinvention." So much of being a creative person means using the same raw materials in a new or unique way to come up with a final result that no one's ever seen before. And then doing it again. And again. And again. To pursue mastery in any field you can't simply reach a certain level of knowledge and then keep repeating what you've always done. You have to reinvent. Your process, your methods, even yourself. This ability to rapidly gain a new perspective, pivot your approach, and change up how you've always done something is key to thinking like an entrepreneur.

Ownership.

To me, this means knowing yourself and embracing full responsibility for your own future. In other words, not expecting any class, program, school, or person to automatically make your dreams happen for you. No entitlement. It's about knowing that it's no one else's responsibility or duty to get you where you need to go is all up to you. And being a self-starter means taking action without waiting for anyone else to hand you anything along the way.

Perseverance. Reinvention. Ownership. Being a "PRO." Blend these together and mix it with your talents and gifts you'll have your brain properly configured for taking action on the things we're talking about in this book. I don't want to get too detailed about what entrepreneurship entails (they have entire Master's programs for that), but I do want to connect some dots between your formal education, career path, personal talents, and unique sense of purpose to show how this way of thinking can benefit you as your pursue your dreams. I guess a few words of caution and clarification may be in order before we really dig in so let me throw a few of those at you as well.

Entrepreneurship is not about:

...chasing money. Not every entrepreneur is rich. Entrepreneurship isn't an idea that's fundamentally about money. If you're feeling some kind of pressure that you have to create and sell a billion dollar start-up then try to think of the word "entrepreneur" as close to its etymological root as you can. From the 1850s Old French, the heart of the word is focused on an "undertaking." In other words, someone who "undertakes or manages."

...inventing technology. We so often hear about entrepreneurs as business leaders who are doing huge things in technology. Social media. AI, VR, energy. These are all great applications of entrepreneurship but don't miss the forest for the trees. This output is just one example of entrepreneurship in action. You can apply your entrepreneurial mind to anything. If it's something you care about, then it counts.

... being born a genius. I've seen a lot of people get discouraged over time when they've tried to pursue their own endeavors. Although most people may not verbalize it, I think there is some conscious or unconscious sense that the people we look to as beacons of entrepreneurship are geniuses. They're just born smarter and more gifted than everyone else. Straight up. I think, actually, I know, this is a myth. Look back up at my list of the 3 ingredients of entrepreneurship. "Innate genius" is not on the list. Neither is "massive intelligence." Some of the most incredible stories of world-changing entrepreneurship were birthed from the minds and actions of "regular" people. Not geniuses. Not people that went to Harvard at 12 years old. Just people.

I hope that as you hear my story and consume these lessons of entrepreneurship that you'll see how perseverance, reinvention, and ownership can be applied to anything and everything in your life to help you crystallize and bring about the creative dreams you have for yourself.

SUMMARY: Entrepreneurship is about being a "P.R.O." aka having Perseverance, Reinvention, and Ownership.

BRAIN DUMP: Do you think of yourself as an entrepreneur? Do you do "entrepreneurial" things? How has this chapter changed your perception on what it means to persevere, reinvent, and own your future?

I'm a YouTube celebrity?

I know we're taking a chronological approach here as we talk about my experiences and the lessons I've learned along the way but in this chapter I want to talk about something that overlaps with a few different times in my life, some of which we've already covered, others of which we have yet to dig into. Basically, over the span of time from youth pastoring to running my own company to working at the law firm, I maintained a small YouTube channel, mostly just for fun and occasional artistic projects that I wanted to document and because I really liked filming and editing video. However, something happened with my channel that would change the role that YouTube played in my life, basically overnight. What was it?

Monetization.

Monetization is a fancy marketing word for "how stuff can make you money." In the case of YouTube videos it means that those ads that play before or during your videos, if clicked, can earn you dollars. Back in the dark ages of YouTube not everyone could just click the "monetization" button on their videos and suddenly start making money from ads. No, back then you had to actually be chosen to be part of the YouTube partner program. This was no small feat and required writing, verification, swearing an oath (kidding), filling out forms, all kinds of ridiculous things that would never fly today. Yet back in the early days of YouTube I was chosen to be a partner and never looked back.

I had a few videos that were really popular. They were terrible quality. Way too grainy. Too much blue. No color correction. Standard definition. Poor framing. Bad music. Too long. But you know what? People all over the world who were searching for something specifically related to my car videos kept finding my work. They'd watch my videos constantly. I kept getting subscribers. I monetized my videos and starting making crazy amounts of money.

How much?

$1.50. Maybe even $3. Per week.

Sure it was barely enough to take my wife out for a classy date at McDonald's but it was real money from something artistic I was doing for fun. To this day this feeling still amazes me because I can't believe that I can get paid and make money for things I love to do. This is the greatest opportunity yet the most difficult challenge for creative people, to accept the reality that work can be both artistically fulfilling and financially prosperous. But perhaps that's for another book. I casually produced YouTube videos here and there (why I didn't do more in the early days of my channel is a mystery to me), continually adding to my body of work and producing more content for the search engine monsters to gobble up.

Fast forward a few years. YouTube is now dominating the social media scene and is the #1 source for online video. YouTube has become a verb. It's a household name. It's acquired by Google. Billions of dollars are falling out of the sky and online video could not be hotter. Now I had always produced my videos with the intent of getting them found in popular searches related to my subject matter (drawing cars, painting cars). I'd be sure to use the right keywords in my video titles and descriptions and purposefully make multi-part videos from the same shoot to try grab as much video real estate as I could. Yet as my follower count grew I began to see more and more comments asking for specific videos and tutorials. They were interested in me and my life. They were saying thanks... and really meant it. People from all over the world.

I started to think about changing my approach from simply making videos for the search engine monsters to gobble up to cultivating a real online community with my followers. This mindset change altered how I approached my channel and the time I planned to spend on it but has proven to be very rewarding both in terms of the monetization of my videos and the sense of satisfaction I have about this "world" I've created in the actual world.

Before we get too serious let me take a moment to talk about all the trolls, negative comments, and even death threats that I got from YouTube. Now if you know anything about social media then you know that trolling and rage-filled comments are par for the course and simply part of the online social media experiment. I had this one video that was half joke/half serious about how to play the guitar by taking off all but 3 strings and tuning them the same. Then all you had to do is touch a fret with your thumb and BOOM! You were making heavy metal or punk rock music. The truth about this video is that it does actually work and I recorded 4 albums using this method back in the day. I never really had the patience to learn all the chords so I just made up my own way that I could play immediately without practicing (hence the video tutorial). But my, oh my, did this make the rock and roll community mad. Like really mad.

At first these comments did hurt. They would say things like how terrible it was and how I didn't deserve to even be making music and how I was an insult to (fill in the blank music genre), etc. A few times yes, people threatened me. On the Internet. Anonymously. And from a foreign country I think.

Whoever they were and however serious they may have been, this did sting in the beginning. Years later I continue to get negative comments (everyone will if you have a video up online) but it just doesn't impact me anymore. I can laugh off any comment on my videos now, something I wasn't always able to do.

As my channel grew I tried more and more things. I ran a contest and sent the winner some gear. I used different cameras. I tried all sorts of different lighting setups, types of editing tricks, longer videos, shorter videos, a merchandise store, website, all kinds of stuff. My greatest limitation was, and continues to be, time. YouTube offered me one-on-one consulting as a service to partners. I went to a YouTube Creators Conference in Washington DC. I bought gear. I replaced my MacBook's screen because all the heat from the constant rendering dried out the glue that held the glass to the lid. And all of this while I continued in my full time job and kept having more kids. And moving at least once (it's all a blur).

Now YouTube has become central to my thinking and planning and a core focus in how I plan and assign my creative free time. I have almost 300 videos I've created, thousands of subscribers, millions of views, and even had a few cool conversations with major brands and channels about sponsorships and features. While none of these sponsor opportunities have panned out I continue to try new things and build my personal brand, looking at my channel analytics for trends and trying to produce as much as I can in my tiny wood-paneled basement that's 90% full of Legos, kids toys, bookshelves and laundry.

So what does this have to do with you? Here are a few lessons I think can apply to anyone.

Take your passions seriously.

A lot of people used to think of YouTube as a fun and recreational kind of tool, like watching TV. Even if you were a creator it wasn't really considered a substantial part of anyone's income stream until the concept of a "YouTube celebrity" became a thing and certain viral videos started to get shown on late night TV and even the news. Now, there are more ways than ever to make money from your side interests. From online sales of homemade knitted hats to ad platforms to selling graphics or videos, the Internet as a direct-to-anyone tool of opportunity has allowed more people than ever to make an income from the passions in their lives that are not their full time careers. So think seriously about your passions and how you might find a win/win with your interests to both bring you income and serve as a creative outlet for you.

Always improve your craft.

No matter if it's dance or painting, poetry or badminton, you need to find that place in your life where you are "aggressively content." In other words, you are aggressive in the pursuit of quality and excellence in your specific area of passion. Yet you are also content and at peace with the time and energy you have available to give to it as well as your pace of improvement. Remember, it's not about being the best at XYZ on the planet. When I went to art school and on the first day realized that although I was the best at drawing cars in my school I was probably the worst at drawing cars from this group of students from all over the world. It's ok to not be the best. It's ok to be content with your progress. Not everything is a competition. Be aggressive. Be content.

If it ain't fun...

This last point is a reminder, perhaps to those of you that are high achievers. You're the students who are crushing all those advanced classes and probably already have a graduate program in mind as well as a short list of places you'd like to work upon graduation. Well, this is for you but really I think a lesson for anyone that produces creative work either for fun or as part of your job. You have to be constantly aware of whether or not you're still having fun. I'm serious. When you are in step with your calling you should be in a place where your default perspective about your work is that it feels less like work and more like fun. Now, there will be times and seasons where you'll have to do things you don't want to do. Some grunt work. Some heavy lifting, conflict, or stress. This isn't what I'm talking about. What I'm talking about is having an ongoing feeling that you're having a good time with your work, be it side projects or your full time gig. This is your personal barometer so that you can know if something is out of alignment. Maybe your work. Maybe you. More on this later.

What's your side thing? Do you have a YouTube channel? Do you make things? Do you love putting on plays, writing fiction, or sculpting? I want you to take a few moments to think about you're the passions and interests you have and answer a few questions about them.

SUMMARY: It's ok to pivot your side work and passions to bring you a stream of income. Some people are more comfortable with this than others but as soon as it stops being fun you should take a pause to figure out why.

BRAIN DUMP: Is what you're considering pursuing as your main course of study or career in the future the same as your side passions or interests? Do you feel like making money off of your passions cheapens them? Would you say you are more inclined to approach your passions from the purely artistic perspective or the making money perspective?

How to get things done

Going back to the concept of an entrepreneur it's important to be reminded of one principle at the heart of everything else. Ownership. Self-starting. Initiative. In this brief chapter I simply want to share with you some of the "make it happen no matter what" principles I've collected over the years that I feel make the most compelling impact when I think about my day. Whether it's making YouTube videos on my own or leading a content marketing team at an agency, these are the nuggets of wisdom that you can learn, apply, and measure almost immediately. In no particular order (and with some references as appropriate), here they are:

- Attack the day's most important project first thing in the morning for 90 minutes without stopping. (Brian Tracy's book *Eat That Frog*)
- The time you have to complete a project is exactly how much time you will need to do it. (Horstman's corollary to Parkinson's law)
- The farther in advance you plan something, the greater the likelihood it will happen. (Basic budgeting)
- Make a year's worth of goals. Then give yourself 6 months to do them all. We usually allow too much time rather than too little.
- However much time is requested for a meeting, make the meeting half that. (Advice from Colin Powell)
- Make passivity your enemy. When you step into a situation, drive it and own it. You'll always regret your inactions more than your actions. Move first.
- Don't have too many goals. Less goals = better chances of getting anything done.
- There will never be a time when all the

circumstances are perfect to start something. Don't wait for that time. It's not coming.

- Focus on one thing for an hour a day and you'll be an expert in a few years.
- Don't wait for permission. If you have obtained a position or role you have the authority to take action.
- Just start. Take the first step. Do something. Your goal at this moment is not completion, it's gaining momentum.

SUMMARY: There are timeless nuggets of wisdom for how to think about your time and how to take control over it. The more you budget it and manage your time, the more it will seem like you have.

BRAIN DUMP: On a scale of 1-10 (1 = terrible, 10 = superstar), how well do you think you budget your time?

Which two items from the above list are ones you think you struggle with?

Which single item from the above list is something you think you could implement in your own life starting tomorrow?

I'm going to work at an ad agency?!

After working at the law firm for almost 2 years I could sense another change in the air. While in my position I was given an incredible amount of freedom and responsibility to try new marketing platforms and strategies, learn not only FDA regulatory law and compliance, but also international SEO and digital marketing. I learned a ton. Over the last decade or so I had been in touch with various mentor figures from a variety of background and one individual, the Chief Creative at a strategic communications firm, I had specifically considered as someone to help guide me to a larger-scale creative career. Specifically, doing something at an ad agency.

I'll take some liberties just for a second to clarify some things about how the "sausage factories" of creative work operate and how they're distinct from each other. Here's a quick breakdown that I think should be helpful to you especially if you're considering a career in the creative disciplines.

Advertising Agency. An advertising agency is sort of what it sounds like. It's a place where advertisements are made. This is partially true although now what's meant by "advertising" is as diverse as ever and includes writing, video, music production, etc. Essentially, an ad agency is a larger organization than a few people, the "big ones" being global brands with international offices. These shops are fast-paced, aggressive, and known for pushing boundaries. Most of the creative work done for everyday brands you love (think Starbucks, Apple, Nike), is produced by one of these larger, international agencies.

Strategic communications firm: Strategic communications can mean a lot of things so to be honest, it depends on the individual firm. Essentially, strategic communications may vary from traditional advertising in that there will be more emphasis placed on research, strategic planning, internal communications, and market positioning. Other times, a strategic communications firm will do everything an advertising agency firm does as well, or utilize vendors and partners for some of the execution. Similarly, a large advertising agency may tap a strategic communications firm for some of their needs on the research, positioning, or branding side.

Public relations firm: A public relations firm is an organization that helps their clients get featured in the news, magazines, online, or TV. At a PR firm you will work with a client to understand their needs and how to find the newsworthy angle of their current situation in order to get them featured on Good Morning America, Gizmodo, Wired, or local TV. It could be any type of client, any placement, with goals varying from a measurable number of website hits or downloads to a broader capture of something called "top of mind awareness" which is fancy marketing speak for people thinking of you when they have a need. While some PR shops will produce their own media and creative they are usually working with other creative shops, media buyers, or freelancers for a lot of the creative execution.

Marketing firm/agency: A marketing firm is a broad term which can also mean a lot of things depending on the shop. Usually a marketing firm will have a greater focus on tools, technologies, and platforms than an agency or PR house. This means that they will have deep expertise in a variety of the deeply technical and tactical sides of advertising and marketing such as email newsletter tools, search engine optimization, pay per click ads and tracking, analytics assessments and reporting, web banner advertising, display advertising, sales funnel and lead tracking, customer relations tools, landing pages, direct response mail, and microsites.

Digital agency: Any marketing, advertising, or PR shop can describe themselves as a "digital" agency. This just means that their focus is primarily on digital tools such as websites, videos, interactive experiences, social media, and email. This is a response to the traditional suite of agency offerings which in the past was focused on print.

Full service agency: An agency that calls themselves "full service" is essentially saying that they can do anything, whether print or digital. This is usually true although a lot of medium and large shops will tap an army of other agencies and freelancers depending on what kind of work is needed and how fast. A full service agency's goal is usually to become Agency of Record (AOR) for a particular brand. This is a bit like a marriage declaration that says to any other firm trying to work with a specific brand that, "Hey, these guys are ours. We do their creative work." A full service agency will say yes to whatever needs or projects a brand will bring them and usually the client is not aware what's done by the agency and what is subbed out to a contractor or freelancer.

Boutique firm/agency: Any PR, advertising, or strategic communications firm can be "boutique" if they are focused strictly on one specific market or industry. For example, you may have some agencies or PR shops that are only focused on sports and athletic clients. Others are only focused on non-profits. Or healthcare. Or higher ed. Being a boutique firm is good on one hand because it communicates to your specific niche that you have deep expertise in their area and with their kinds of needs. Other times it can be a disadvantage if there are a lot of other competitors in your space, if the market opportunity changes, or if there's a recession or major cut back in that field.

Publishing house: A publishing house is different than everything else above. A publishing house is just what it sounds like, an organization that publishes books and magazines. I include it here because many creative people with strong writing abilities often find themselves involved with a publishing house at some point in their career and knowing how they work and the roadmap that's needed to move ideas to a published work can be very helpful. A publishing house may engage with a marketing firm to promote a book or author but usually not a larger agency. Oftentimes they have staff to do the creative in house.

Whew, that's a lot of options. Essentially, you'll be able to search online and quickly find the larger shops. They'll have a main office in a major city with international locations at the big hub cities such as London or Tokyo. For the rest of the medium-sized marketing, PR, and creative shops, each region will have some major players but with countless smaller shops saturating every inch of the USA and beyond. There is a lot of really great work being done by shops of 10 – 20 people and in the last few years a lot of these smaller shops have started to work with major brands and receive some much-deserved recognition for their accomplishments.

All in all it's a really cool time to be doing creative work. If you decide to go the agency route (as opposed to being on an in-house creative team within an organization itself), there are a few things you should know. But instead of talking any more in abstractions, how about just joining me on my journey into agency life? Here we go.

I never used to be a flashy dresser.

Throughout high school and college I wore jeans, Velcro tennis shoes and a black hoodie. Not the same black hoodie mind you... Well, maybe it was the same one. I basically lived in it. When I got married my wife pushed me out of my comfort zone in some new and surprising ways. I had my first cup of coffee with her. It was a café mocha. At Starbucks. My mind exploded. Now I'm up to 500 cups of coffee per day. Yet one of the most tangible ways that Robin pushed me was in my personal style (or lack thereof). While we both were into punk rock and harder music I did have to break away from my standard jeans/hoodie motif, especially as I gained more responsibility and did more "business stuff" as part of my day job. One day we were at a store and I jokingly pulled a pair of bright red dress pants off the rack to show Robin. The conversation went like this.

> Me: "Hey, do you think I should get these? Hahah."
>
> Robin: "You should totally get those pants. They are awesome."
>
> Me: "Hahahah."
>
> Robin: "I'm serious. You need those red pants."
>
> Me: "What?"
>
> Cashier: "With your coupon today that will be $55.95, will you be paying cash or credit?"

So my wife talked me into buying bright red dress pants. My first day at this creative agency it was snowing. I wore my bright red pants. I knew at that moment that I had stepped into a new phase of my life.

Agency life is demanding. It's fun. It's fast. You will often need to build the plane while you're flying it. You'll need to maintain an air of confidence with your clients while simultaneously knowing that you have no idea what the solution will be or how it's going to get done. But you're creative. You ARE a creative. This is what you do. The rhythm of agency life is the outcome of what happens when you try to constantly marry opposing forces and integrate them. Those forces are:

- Free flowing creative imagination vs. non-negotiable deadlines
- The purity of art vs. the research of what makes people act
- The enjoyment of creative teams vs. the stress of creative teams
- The stability of going with what you know works vs. the constant need to experiment with new ideas
- The need to master tools and technologies vs. the need for constant learning and innovation.
- The desire to make your clients happy and do what they ask vs. the need to push your clients and tell them that what they want is wrong.
- Focusing on an industry or niche vs. serving

all types of clients
- Following your heart (right brain) vs. leveraging your mind (left brained)

I think you get the idea. The good news is that dealing with the tensions between the different polarities of agency life sharpens you and makes you better in ways you never thought possible. You'll throw yourself into the murky depths of the creative waters and be forced to swim. But you love this. And so do your coworkers. And usually your clients understand this too and, if you're as fortunate as I was to have some really outstanding clients, you'll walk through the process together and learn as you go.

So back to my first day. Red pants. Didn't know anyone. Moving away from law into hardcore creative work. Huge green screen studio. Expensive cameras. Everyone working on Apple products. Fonts and artwork everywhere. For a creative person, this is heaven. You've found your people. For the next five years I threw myself into agency life. I feel really fortunate to work at a shop that had a great work/life balance and wasn't asking me to die on the hill of each project and work 20,000 hours each week. Every day I would learn something from other people, from my own research, from a client, from an article or blog.

It's like I was being paid to learn and improve my craft, the output being work that made my clients happy and the process involving other cool creative people who were into the same things I was. Here are a few stories I recall from agency life that I think are probably similar to the tales that many will have who have been through a stint at an agency.

I remember countless meetings where we would listen to clients and their needs and propose a solution. Oftentimes I can recall the exact moment when I could see on their faces that a light bulb had gone on in their mind. These are deeply satisfying moments.

I remember tons of free food. It just flowed endlessly. Agencies will do a lot of wooing and romancing of clients to get their work so I can't tell you have many leftover plates of sandwiches, charcuterie, bagels, and cheese plates I snagged. Some weeks I could remember only bringing lunch one day because all the other days had some form of free food with them. This is a great perk.

I remember the feeling of when a project was completed. What we dreamed up on a whiteboard a few months was now a real "thing" and out in the world. Maybe it was a website or marketing brochure, a social media campaign, or video. Regardless of what it was, when you're part of the process of bringing something beautiful into the world when before there was nothing… this is the rush of the creative process. It's what creative people live for.

I remember sometimes when things didn't go so well. I messed something up for a client. We dropped the ball. Our client wasn't happy. Someone on my team wasn't. Those were never fun days but I sought to keep them in perspective and remind myself of two things. First, I am not perfect and I will make mistakes. Second, being part of something great means that the people around you will also make mistakes and therefore continue to accept you when it's your turn to fumble.

I remember spontaneous moments. With an open floor plan and 70+ creatives all working in close proximity, spontaneous fun is bound to happen. I remember Nerf gun battles, random clapping, musical serenades, surprise pizza parties, a finer things club, hot sauce challenge, jam sessions, rap battles, dance offs, cubicle pranks, indoor bike rides, and rubber chickens.

I remember seeing the creative work of others and being so blown away that I assumed I would never be able to create work like that. Later down the road I would suddenly realize that I was teaching others to do the things I learned myself just a year or two earlier.

I remember inspiring students. We would often have high school or college students over to our super-creative space for tours and workshops and I loved these times, to be able to do just what I'm doing now: share my story. I know that for some of these students our time together opened doors and ideas they never considered until they experienced what we did at our agency.

I remember learning about new industries like cybersecurity, human resources, banking, healthcare, and recruiting.

I remember the day that I had the revelation about the heart and soul of what this book is about. Many things in my life crystallized on the ride to work or home or while at my desk (where I may have been working.)

I love that people who knew me couldn't believe that my job was my job. I remember going to a junior high career day and telling the students that I basically was on Twitter all day for my job. It's something that can be hard and tedious but everyone at an agency should savor the fact that this work can be so fun. Not everyone has this experience as part of their primary job.

Years passed at the agency. I started a content marketing line of business which grew and became very successful. I learned how creative work was done in the federal government. I learned how organizations tracked time and profit. I learned how to ask for mentorship and receive it. I learned how to manage and lead a team and attempt to find that sweet spot of accountability and freedom, of inspiration and task-management. I learned so much. I still am learning. I think the longer you're at a creative agency the more you'll get the feeling that there's so much you don't know. Even when invited to speak at marketing events and conferences you'll be thinking, "Why did they ask me, I don't really know anything."

Everyone's self-assessment of their own skillsets and proficiency is relative. It can be relative to people they know who are far more advanced and talented. It can be relative to much junior people who are just starting out. It can be relative to a former version of themselves. Any way you slice it there is one great temptation in the creative industries and that is to primarily think about your own creative identity by comparing yourself to someone else.

Just don't.

Stop it.

Thankfully this is a lesson I was fortunate enough to learn early on, although this is one of those "big picture lessons" where you never really finish the learning process. You simply become better at constantly re-learning the same lesson over and over. The lesson here is about comparison. It's about self-identity. It's about having confidence in yourself and your creative output all while knowing that you are not the best in the world at something. You may not be the best in your state. Or at your workplace. Or in your department. This is ok. Talent isn't everything. In fact, it's less than half. As a follower of Jesus I felt free to not have to find my identity in being creative. Or successful. Or perfect. It's not always easy to do because I like to be recognized for my work and accomplishments. Yet the more notches on my creative belt and the more people I meet the more I realize that I can't place the burden of my self-identity on anything else in the universe except God. Not even on myself. And not in my art.

I'll explain this more later but for now, let me ask you a few questions that I think will help you as may be thinking about whether a career in a creative agency is right for you.

SUMMARY: Learn as much as you can wherever you can. If you find yourself at a creative agency enjoy the ride, accept the demands, get past the stumbling blocks and don't compare yourself or your work to others when it comes to your own identity.

BRAIN DUMP: Do you see yourself working at a creative agency in the future? Or for a specific brand or company? Or perhaps being a freelancer? Describe what you imagine here:

Do you do your best creative work in teams or more on your own with the team elements in the beginning or end of a project?

Are you recharged by large groups of people and activity or do you need to be completely alone in order to "charge up your batteries?"

How to give a great presentation

A major component of life as an entrepreneur often comes down to persuasively communicating ideas and concepts to others. This is certainly the case at an agency. Sometimes it's in the form of a slick image-driven website. Other times it's in person over a cup of coffee. Yet more often than not, it's in the form of the dreaded presentation! Maybe it's PowerPoint or just you and a whiteboard, yet whatever form it may take, the ability to give a decent presentation in front of other people is a skill that many fear, some enjoy, and few master. Thankfully for all of us my goal here is not to attempt to make you a master presenter so that you can take the main stage for a TED talk. Instead, I want you to consider these insights about giving presentations the next time you have one.

Prep, prep, prep

This goes first because everything you're about to read is based on this groundwork. You can't finish your presentation, save it on a thumb drive, rush into an event and wow your audience. It just doesn't work that way. If you've seen presentations or TED talks that seem casual, effortless, and unscripted, you can be sure that the presenters rehearsed and revised their talk about a million times. This is how it's done. Practice. Prepare. Over prepare. Rehearse it. Tweak it. Time it. Film it. By the time you're ready to actually present in real life you should know your material cold.

Never apologize, disclaim or show your hand.

The worst thing you can do when giving a presentation is start off by saying "I'm not very prepared for this so bear with me," or "I've been sick so sorry if I'm a little off today." Don't show your hand. Don't apologize. Don't cheapen what you're about to say by subconsciously telling your audience that you're going to bore them. Come out strong, act prepared (even if you're not), and please stop disclaiming and apologizing before you even get started. No one knows the backstory. Everyone thinks you're prepared. No one cares if you've been sick. Just get out there and start.

Get moving

What's worse than a boring presentation? A boring presentation where someone stands at the podium the entire time without moving. You have to get moving! Whatever your stage is, walk around it. Take three steps, talk for a bit, then take three steps somewhere else. Just remember the number three. Three minutes then take three steps. Repeat. But watch out: You're going to want to drift back to that podium because subconsciously it's acting as a physical shield between you and your audience. Don't let it. Get away from it. Shun it (more on this later).

Keeping track of time

Here's a good rule of thumb... However long you think you've been talking, it's actually been three times that. Yes, it's true. There is a rip in the space/time continuum between where people sit and listen to you in the audience and where you speak from the front. So be aware that if you think you're taking too long, you definitely are. So have a watch or clock. Don't mention it. Just glance at it. And work backward from when you need to be done. Everyone loves a presentation that ends early so shoot to end early from the get go.

Slide deck do's and dont's

How do you know if your presentation deck is well put together? Quite simply, if it makes sense without you having to be there then it's not a presentation... it's a report. Your presentation deck is there to support what you say, not the other way around. You are the star, not your PowerPoint. Use powerful images and a few words in your presentation deck. Skip the full sentences and bullet points. Use your own verbal communication to transmit your message and have the presentation deck in the background to support it with powerful imagery and key words.

No fig leaves

The less physical barriers there are between you and your audience, the greater the sense of connection you will have. But you know what? We subconsciously protect ourselves from the stage by hanging onto as many barriers as we can. From clinging to a notebook to crossing our arms or hands, these subconscious actions are self-protection triggers that our nerves force us to do…because we feel vulnerable. And there is no greater barrier than that giant, looming, fortress of a table called the podium. Avoid it. Move it away. Don't touch it. Don't lean on it. Don't even look at it.

How to own the stage

If you want to put your audience to sleep then stand in the same place and talk. If you want to keep your audience engaged then move around, be unpredictable, and get up in their space. Don't pace like a tiger but don't stand still. If you're working your presentation deck then move somewhere new every few slides.

What to do with your hands

Fiddling. Jiggling keys. Jiggling change in your

pocket. Nervously fidgeting with a book, notes, or.. stuffed animal. The answer to what to do with your hands is always "nothing." Nothing, except to gesture and interact with your audience on the actual presentation content. No pockets. No change. No fiddling. Props are ok but just use them sparingly.

Script vs Freestyle

Should you actually type out what you're going to say or just "wing it?" Well, those aren't your only two options for how to prepare. I think the third way is the best and that's to have a well-rehearsed freestyle approach. Unless you're giving a formal speech to the President, the United Nations, or as part of an awards presentation, I think you'll be most natural if you're not standing there reading something verbatim (again, why are you there if someone can just read your content?)

Notes: The good the bad and the ugly

Have you ever seen a TED talk where someone used notes? Or note cards? Nope. I'm not saying that you never need notes but if you look at the most compelling presentations out there, the presenters know their stuff. They don't need notes. As you work up to being a Master of the Universe presenter it's ok to use some subtle note cards, but just a few tips. Don't mention your notes or point them out. Write just a few words or phrases per card to get your memory activated, not the entire script. You don't need cards for "Hello, I'm so happy to be here..." so just have notes for the hard stuff.

Your eyes tell the story. Where to look

Remember, it feels 100 times more uncomfortable for you as the presenter than it does for those in the audience. So relax about it. If you make eye contact with people in the audience it only feels weird for you. So look at people. Look at them in the front row. Left side. Right side. But here's the secret sauce. If you talk primarily to the people in the back of the room it will seem like you're engaging with everyone. And thankfully for you the folks in the back are harder to see so it makes it all around less awkward. Look to the back, look left, look right, look up front. But if you're freaking out then just stare at the back row of people and forget everyone else.

Is your audience with you?

If people start fidgeting, checking their phones, or are staring off into space (or the floor), you have lost them. If you notice this happening then you have to disrupt the moment. Shake them up. Do something unexpected. You could simply stop talking and wait and see who perks up. You could walk right into the audience. You could say, "Are you with me?" or "what do you think?" Find a detour that disrupts the presentation and run with it to snap people back. And then you better make it more interesting.

Prep, prep, prep

Prepare a lot. Once you have your outline and slides, sit down, put the computer in presentation mode, and run through it with your real words in your mind. Or out loud. Try it with no notes to see where you're forgetting things. Make sure you know how long per slide. And do it over and over again. Do it out loud, in your mind, it doesn't matter. But run through it again and again. By the time you do it in real life it should feel like deja vu. Kind of like the feeling you're having now since I already made this point earlier on in this chapter.

Advanced Ninja Tips!

If you're a fast learner or just want to get right to the Pro version of my tips then take a look at this. It's a way to quickly make a presentation more engaging and enrich your delivery of it by applying the number three to everything you do in it. Let me show you:

- Three Points: Make your presentation have 3 major points.
- Three Sub-points: If your presentation has lots of details then have only 3 subpoints per point.
- Three Steps: Between delivering each main point, take 3 slow strides across the stage.
- Three Second pauses: When you summarize anything wait 3 seconds before you say that important statement or idea.

SUMMARY: There are a few universal rules for making great presentations to people. If you get better at giving presentations you will be able to leverage that as an advantage in any field you pursue.

BRAIN DUMP: What one word comes to mind when you think about giving presentations to people? (terror, excitement, fear, etc.) Do you think of yourself as a good presenter? Which two tips from the above list really stood out as things you could apply as part of your next presentation at work or school?

I'm going to write a book?!

We've come to a point in this book now where we're just about caught up to the present. I hope you've enjoyed reading the stories about my professional and artistic journey and have had some time to chew on the questions I've served up at the end of each chapter. I've titled this chapter "I'm going to write a book?!" because I think it describes the latest professional evolution in my life, one that isn't even tied to an employer or a company, but more about something that happened in my own brain that led to this book.

In the past, some of my favorite moments have been when I've had the opportunity to tell my story.

I remember sitting on a panel discussion at Loyola University talking about social media ethics and having the opportunity to explain how my Bible and Theology degree related to my automotive design which related to my YouTube work which related to my ad agency experiences. In moments like those I feel like my story really opens a lot of doors for conversation and gives strength to those who may have a similar story in terms of their past careers and education not making the most sense. I felt that since this was what I really cared about and enjoyed talking about that I would go ahead and write a book about it. Which I did. Which you're reading. Thank you.

I feel like life is more like a circle than a line. If you travel along far enough you'll see that the path you're on is a very long curve, like the surface of the earth, and not a straight and endless road at all. Go along it for a really long time and you'll find that you recognize some of the surroundings, because you've made a complete circle and have come back to where you started. This isn't a bad thing, as if there's no progress in life or that we're meant to spin in circles, it just means that our lives have a rhythm, a sense of cycle, that often will bring us back to a familiar place.

For me, I found that my journey did indeed bring me to a familiar place. It was a place I had known all along and that really I brought with me wherever I went. Just like if you are in a very large maze and you unwind a spool of thread as you go through it, eventually you'll find the places you've been when you turn a corner and see the thread you left there before. Thankfully life isn't a maze but the idea is still the same. God is weaving a common thread through your past, present, and future. This thread is unique to you, and it saturates everything you do. Sometimes you feel like your specific thread is very obvious and that everyone can see it. Other times it's as if there's no thread at all and you feel like you are wandering in the dark with no map or compass.

My "thread" has been creative communication. In automotive design I communicated the feel and shape of a car through marker and chalk. As a Youth Pastor I used words, experiences, and relationships to creatively communicate the deep truths of the Bible and to help students learn it. When running my own business I learned to creatively communicate through web design, video, graphics, and social media. In legal marketing I did the same but also through the barriers of other cultures and languages. In the creative agency I experienced the purity of creative communication through persuasive writing, branding, web content, and in-person events. Now with this book I have the privilege of looking back and seeing that creative thread (it's always easier looking backward), and sharing about it so that you can be encouraged that God is weaving a unique thread through your story as well.

So. What's your creative thread?

Where do you see your past connecting to your present? What from your childhood is playing out now in your school? Or in your job? What's the song that all of your past experiences are singing?

You may not have a clue. But you may have a hunch. Yet I believe that if you look for the thread and believe that you'll find it, you will. And once you do, you'll be able to delight in the fact that you are here on this earth with a purpose, with a unique set of gifts and talents, a unique role and circle of influence. This is my challenge to you and if I can help, I will.

But enough about me. This book is really about you.

SUMMARY: Things often make sense only when you look back on them. The secret is to move forward with excitement, confidence, and expectation, even if you're not really sure of the way.

BRAIN DUMP: Which chapter or concept in this book really got you thinking? Why?

What are two takeaways from this book that you can immediately apply to your life?

Do you feel like you have more tools in your personal toolbox now than when you first picked this book up?

It's your time now

Well, this is officially the last chapter of the book. I hope you've learned a few things and been inspired to act on them. I hope my personal story has served as fuel for your dreams, at least in the sense that if I could go from cars to church to entrepreneur to legal to advertising then anything is possible for you. I hope you've picked up from my story some combination of the following truths:

- Although it sounds like it all makes sense looking backward, I had no idea it would all play out this way.
- I don't regret any of the choices that led me from one career path to the next. I think God inspired and led me to take the leap each time it was needed.

- My family has supported me at every turn. Whether my parents when I decided to change schools, my wife when I wanted to go out on my own, or my kids when I ask them to participate in some crazed art project. This would be a very different story without their support.

- Every major decision in my life has been an emotional blend of excitement, fear, questioning, and anticipation. I think having a good blend of risk, confidence, and wisdom is essential for owning your own professional growth.

- I invested the time to write this book because one of the most rewarding things in my life is to share my story and see others be inspired to chase their own dreams. I hope you've been inspired in some way to chase yours.

- I believe that entrepreneurship is now the most vital skill set needed to thrive in the digital age. Whether you work for a global corporation or do your own thing, we live in an age of individual possibility where anyone can do anything. Once you understand this and start taking ownership over your own entrepreneurial spirit, you'll start making huge leaps forward.

I titled this chapter "It's Your Time Now" because I want you to write your own next chapter. Take what I've shared and run with it. Keep the story going. Focus on your next step. But don't slow down. Don't let up. If you're inspired and on fire then go. Make it happen. Charge ahead.

Yet if this seems like a lot to process and you're just trying to finish school, get a summer job, or make it until the weekend, I get it. Don't let the simple and succinct storytelling of this book fool you into thinking that I sat down according to a "plan" and made this all happen. I didn't. And there were long chunks of time where it felt like nothing was happening at all. When I wasn't motivated. I had no idea what was next. There have been some very bad days. There have been a ton of really great days. And in between those polar opposites, a lot of days. Just regular days. Routines. The grind.

And you know what? That's ok.

I remember reading an article years ago called *The Glory of the Grind*. It was about how so much of the best parts of life are actually the sum of simple, everyday, non-spectacular days. So we shouldn't neglect these ordinary days. Or try to force them all to be mountain top days. What is required is to keep our eyes on the prize, our feet on the ground, and our hearts attuned to the good that we have. For me this has been a process of walking with God through every stage and phase of life I've experienced since becoming a follower of Jesus. So much of the peace that I have and the confidence I tap into comes not *from* me but *to* me. And through me. From God and His power at work in me. This is my greatest hope for you if you've made it to the end of the book, for you to have that same peace and joy that lets you run free wherever your calling takes you. Because if you have a "calling" it means Someone is doing the calling. And it's not you. Think about it.

I wish you the best. Now go create an amazing future!

About the Author

A true creative communicator, Jon has experienced enough seemingly disconnected careers in his short lifetime to confuse any guidance counselor. Charging ahead with the realization that creativity can be applied to any profession, Jon currently works at Maryland-based ADG Creative where he leads a thriving content marketing practice with clients in cyber, HR, banking, architecture, executive search, and telecom. Speaking frequently on all things content, digital, viral and creative, Jon has run his own advertising and design firm, worked with youth in the non-profit sector, and run marketing for a regulatory consulting firm and legal practice dedicated to helping clients succeed in FDA regulatory compliance. His YouTube channel has millions of views with videos on car design, filmmaking, creativity, and other assorted mayhem. His finest work has involved unicorns and trade show pranks, hand-painted car murals, meteorological impostering, fictional office park war heroes, car design, executive ghost writing, and ancient Greek. He holds an Undergraduate Degree in Theology from Washington Bible College, a Master's Degree in Modern Studies from Loyola University Maryland, and after flirting with a doctoral program eventually decided that making YouTube videos was a better investment of energy. A long time Maryland resident Jon lives with his wife Robin and 4 boys in Ellicott City, MD.

Apprentice
House Press
Loyola University Maryland

Apprentice House is the country's only campus-based, student-staffed book publishing company. Directed by professors and industry professionals, it is a nonprofit activity of the Communication Department at Loyola University Maryland.

Using state-of-the-art technology and an experiential learning model of education, Apprentice House publishes books in untraditional ways. This dual responsibility as publishers and educators creates an unprecedented collaborative environment among faculty and students, while teaching tomorrow's editors, designers, and marketers.

Outside of class, progress on book projects is carried forth by the AH Book Publishing Club, a co-curricular campus organization supported by Loyola University Maryland's Office of Student Activities.

Eclectic and provocative, Apprentice House titles intend to entertain as well as spark dialogue on a variety of topics. Financial contributions to sustain the press's work are welcomed. Contributions are tax deductible to the fullest extent allowed by the IRS.

To learn more about Apprentice House books or to obtain submission guidelines, please visit www.apprenticehouse.com.

Apprentice House
Communication Department
Loyola University Maryland
4501 N. Charles Street
Baltimore, MD 21210
Ph: 410-617-5265 • Fax: 410-617-2198
info@apprenticehouse.com • www.apprenticehouse.com

CPSIA information can be obtained
at www.ICGtesting.com
Printed in the USA
FFHW02n0627090918
48255288-52020FF